Fat Girls

Hot Sexy Fat Lingerie Girls Models Pictures

By EROTICA PHOTO ART LOVER

Copyright © Fat Girls

All rights reserved. No part of this document may be
Reproduced or transmitted in any form or by any means, electronic, mechanical, photocopying,
Recording, or otherwise, without prior written permission of erotica photo art lover.

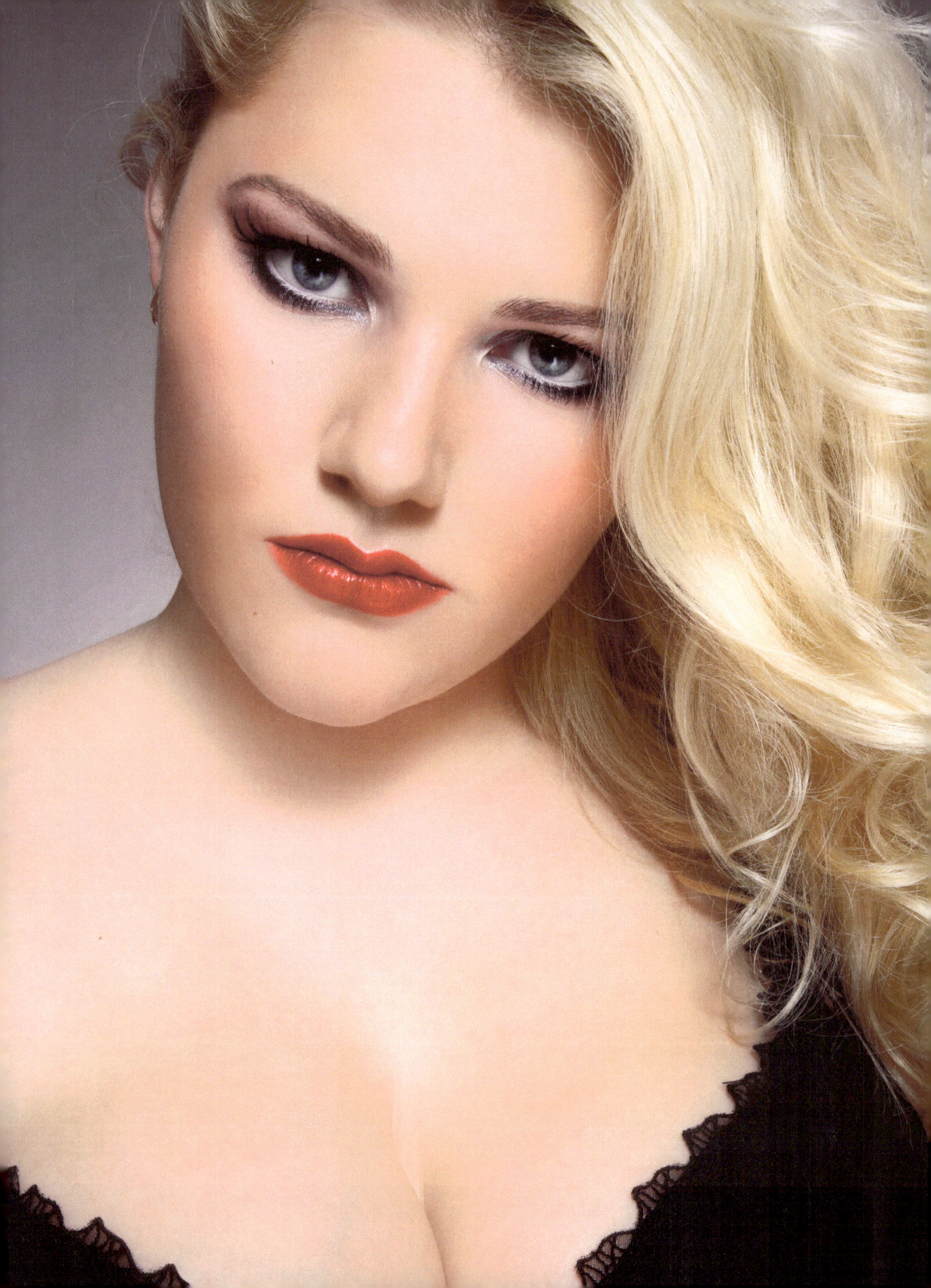

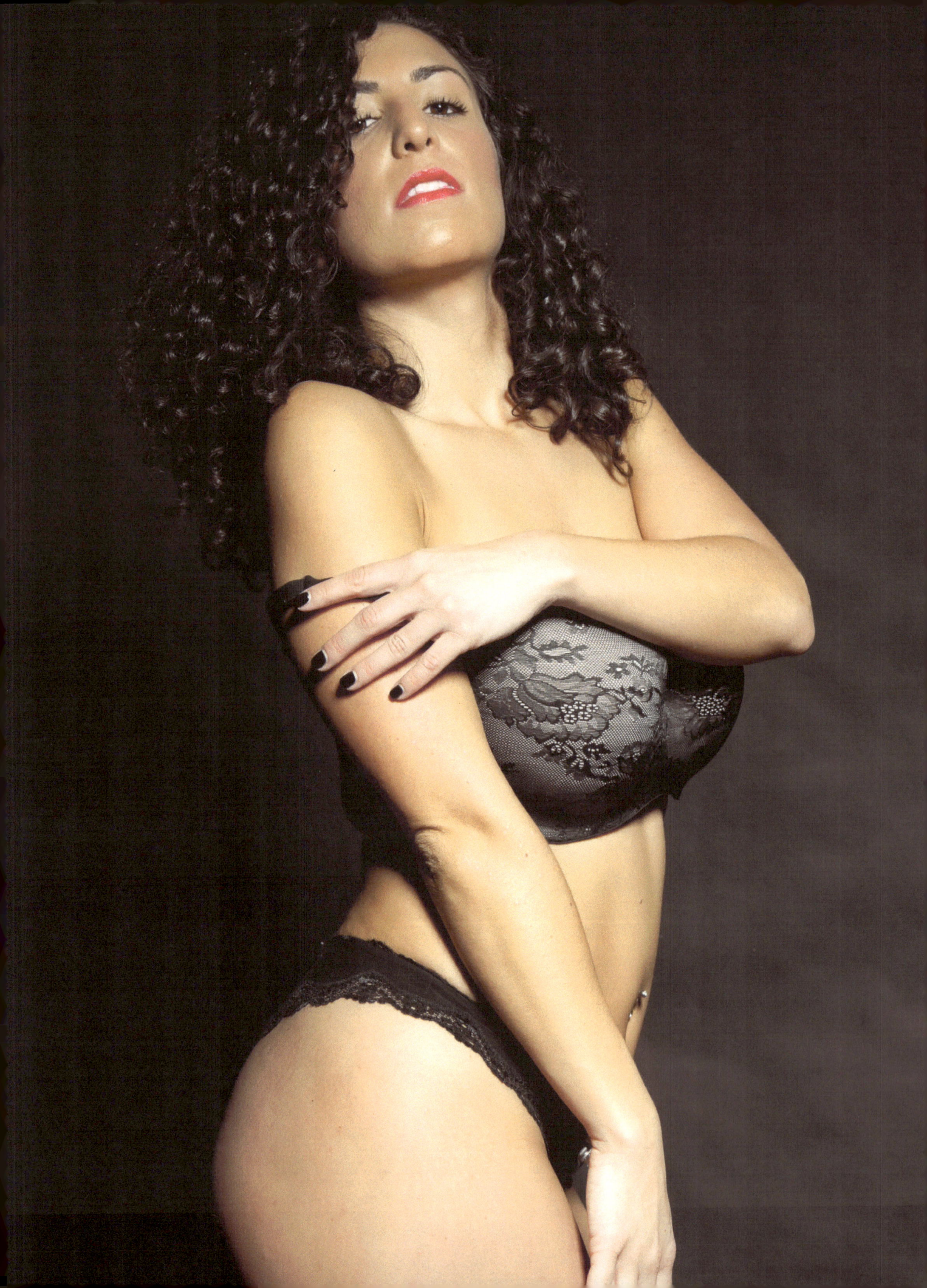

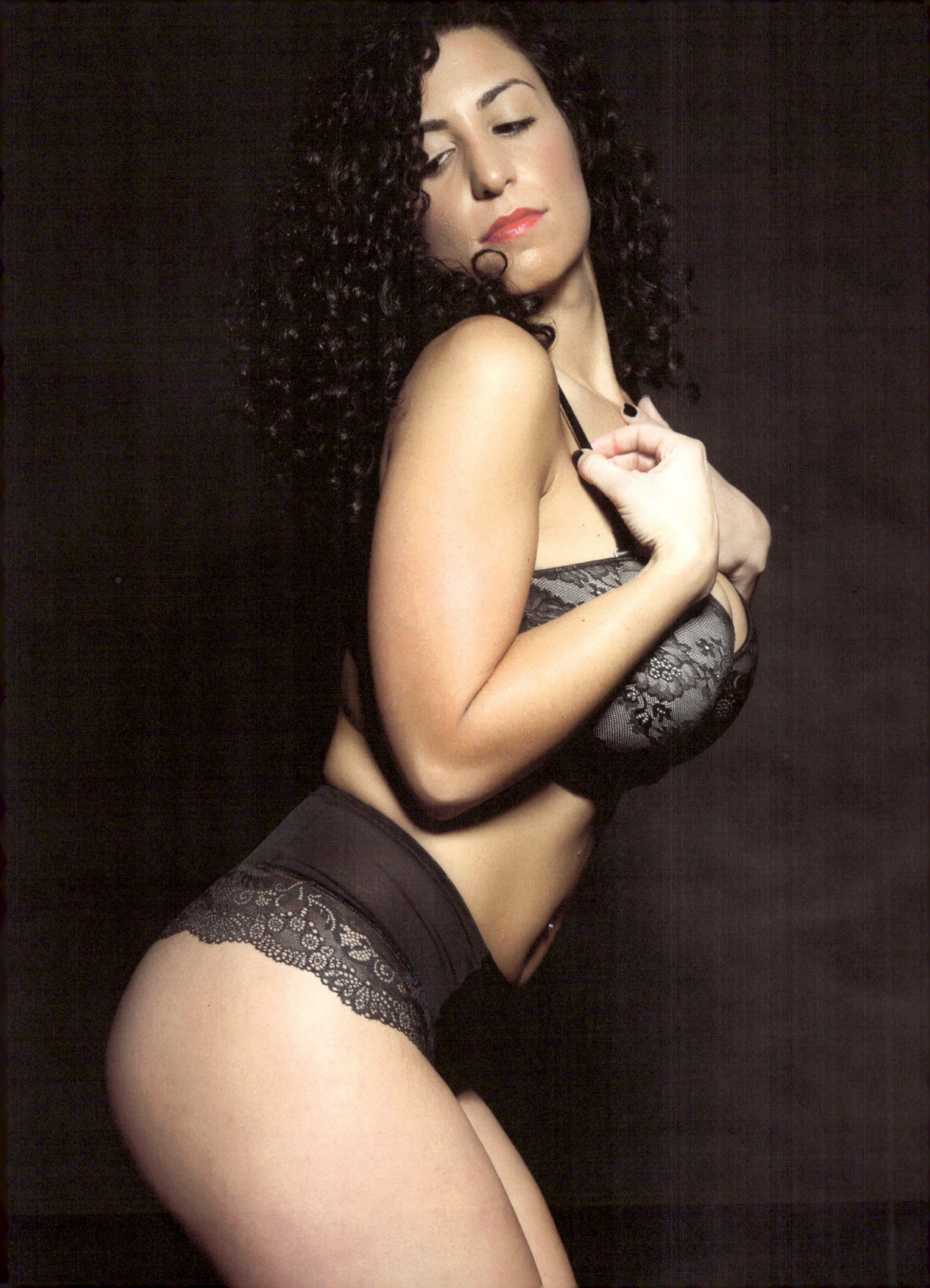

www.ingramcontent.com/pod-product-compliance
Lightning Source LLC
Chambersburg PA
CBHW050419180526
45159CB00005B/2330